THE DIARY OF A BRIDE TO BE

BOOK 2
THE RETURN OF SPRING

KATANDRA SHANEL JACKSON

FreedomInk

PO Box 161965 Atlanta, GA 30321

FreedomInk

Copyright 2012 by Katandra Shanel Jackson
All rights reserved. No part of this publication may be reproduced or transmitted in any form or by any means, electronic or mechanical, including photocopy, recording, or any information storage and retrieval system, without permission in writing from the copyright owner.

Cover design by Elaina Lee.
Page layout by FreedomInk Publishing.
Proofread by Donna Jean Bennett.
Final edit by Katandra Shanel Jackson.

ISBN 978-0-98510-418-4

Printed in the United States of America

http://www.freedomink365.com

PREFACE

FROM THE ASHES... I'M FREE

THE THING I LOVE MOST ABOUT HIM IS THAT HE IS NEVER SUFFOCATING. WE'RE NOT SOME 2 HEADED, YOU BREATHE OUT I BREATHE IN, FREAK OF A THING IN SO CALLED "LOVE". NO. WITH HIM I'VE GROWN FROM SPARROW TO EAGLE TO PHOENIX. HE HAS GIVEN ME WINGS AND IN HIS LOVE I AM FREE.

ACKNOWLEDGEMENTS

I can't say thank you enough to those that add depth in abundance to my life...

To my heavenly angels; Trevon, Kailyn and Ashley. Parenthood is a tricky thing. Children don't come with manuals or do-over buttons. I'm thankful for your resilience, your patience and your understanding. Thank you for loving me, especially when I'm doing my best to get it right! For this I love you.

Best of wishes to my brother, Javar Byrd and his beautiful new bride, Brooke! You two have made me realize that no matter how long it takes for hearts to evolve to the point of being on the same page, it is worth the wait. You two are my Happily Ever After inspiration! I love you.

Many thanks as I am immensely appreciative of each Author that resides at FreedomInk. You all keep me sane as I find the balance between Author and Publisher. You are my surrogate family and I cherish each and every member! I love you.

Herman, thank you for the kisses night after night as you retired and I stayed behind to type just a few more pages. Your tolerance astounds me. And yes, I'm the first to admit, loving me is no easy task. Yet you do it effortlessly. Even when my body is absent, I'm always right there; loving you, as you love me.

You Gals deserved a page all your own...

Special accolades...

To my bestie, Donna Jean, thank you for being super meticulous when it comes to my work. Not a single comma is out of place. I think this particular quirk of yours, have allowed you to accept me whole heartedly. The miles between us are no match for our kinship, sisters by force because this is where life chose for us to be.

To my comrade in arms, Yvette Porter Moore. Not only do you reside at FreedomInk with so many other amazing Authors, but you are a dear friend and my acting mentor. Thanks for always 'keeping it real'. No matter what the situation, you've never sugar coated a thing. If ever I feel myself deviating from the script, I can usually bounce back with an 'Okaaaaaaay!'

To my Twin, Tanja Robinson. No we never shared the same womb, but Honey, it feels like we share the same soul. I could never begin to describe our friendship. A million words wouldn't do. Besides, we never leave a paper trail.

To my Mother, Vernice Scott. Thanks for wearing down this path. The journey has not been easy, but because of you, I know the way. Sorry for being such a brat during my teenage years. Thanks for being such a Fox and for loving little ol' me, more and more each year, even if I have been 29, 5 times. I'm YOUR Lady Day.

Angel Wings

Dr. Darcova Triplett, STRUT! The Magazine,
Las Vegas Nevada & Atlanta Georgia

Latressa Crawford, Sensational Jireh Fashion
Accessories & More, Atlanta Georgia

Mandy Sharpe, Sharpest Image Photography,
Augusta Georgia

Tiffany Leonard, Tiffany's Delectables,
Antioch California

Janette Simone, Simone & KoZ, Oakland California

Trinette T'Shon Collier, California Dreaming Events,
Atlanta Georgia

Stacy Bohannon
Michelle Newham Mobley
Yvette Porter Moore
Javar and Brooke Byrd
Kimberly Kelley
Nancy Grimes
Tanja Robinson

In order for a dream to come true, one must believe in themself. Still, a little help from others is a major blessing. Once again I'm grateful for the graceful breeze delivered by 'Angel' wings...

Thank you,

Kat.

DEDICATION

I dedicate this book to love...

A LETTER TO THE READER

Dear Reader,
Not everything makes sense all of the time and when they don't, isn't it grande to have someone there. Helping you understand, fixing that which you cannot, and always making everything alright. To be grateful for a friendship that deepens in love more and more each day, especially on those that are not as great. In each other's presence you become better. Teaching and learning what it means to truly be free, each day a new experience. Then one day you realize, this is not the beginning, nor are we nearing the end. This is but a piece of the puzzle. The puzzle which is complete as days come full circle in the life of a bride to be. As promised, there has been some stormy weather along the way, but life has taught us to prepare. This time we go in with umbrella at the ready. Nary a knight or princess will let a little rain halt the journey, so it continues! This story is for you……

The Diary of A Bride To Be… Book 2

Katandra Shanel…

FOREWORD

Recap: Most of you know the beginning of this story. For those of you who don't know. Yes, Herman and I met online via Mocospace, and I reiterate *IT IS NOT* 1915. I had just joined and virtual pimp here had over 1,000 "friends". I almost declined the friend request thinking, 'I know exactly what this city player wants'. But just to prove to him that I wasn't some hillbilly from an unknown place, well that last part is true... whoever heard of a Manassas Georgia? Anywho, I accepted the request and the journey has been in motion ever since. Honestly, I didn't think he and I would ever meet. On one hand you have me, this sweet girl from the country. Born and raised in between Claxton (the Fruitcake Capital) & Vidalia (the Sweet Onion Capital). Then you have him, Mr. Atl381 from Atlanta G-A. Home of the Braves, Coca Cola, and the infamous Blue Flame Lounge.

INTRODUCTION

At the end of book 1, I had undergone several transformations, most of them mental. Not only has my state of mind been altered, but wedding details have been tweaked as well... the date, the style of dress, the color scheme, a few members of the wedding party, the location, and the level of peace amongst love birds. My trust, sanity, and security have all been tested. Tempers have soared and bad news has come a knockin'. The discovery of an unresolved divorce was soul crushing. So with all of these elements lingering in my rearview, book 2 begins with Starting Anew.

DISCLOSURE

The recollections recorded in 'The Diary of A Bride To Be' are the sole remembrances of the author, and the author alone. They in no way reflect the opinions of those whose names have been purposely dismissed. All third party names have been omitted to protect the privacy of all that are directly and indirectly involved.

                                        Katandra Shanel...

Table of Contents

Preface	3
Acknowledgements	5
Special Thanks	7
Dedication	9
A Letter to the Reader	11
Foreword	13
Introduction	15
Disclosure	17
Soliloquy	21
Spring	25
Summer	73
Fall	105
Winter	129
Sneak Peek	161

SOLILOQUY

In order to understand the story, sometimes we must begin at the end...

A WEEK OF FEELINGS CAPTURED

Day 1--- Today I am mad, upset, angry, hurt, lost, confused, relieved, miserable and a host of other undesirable emotions are mine. But shock is setting in and replacing all of the above, and the nagging questions, "How... Why?" just keep booming in my ear. Then again, that could be my heart breaking with each beat, with every step he takes, as he walks away.

Day 2--- Today I feel sick. Despite my cool outer appearance, I don't feel so well. All the words from the night before keep repeating in my head, crowding every other thought out, making it impossible to function. I stayed in bed until the sun was high in the sky. Nauseous to say the least. He said he's coming back home, but I'm not really sure what that means. I'm not really sure if I can forgive him.

Day 3--- Not much in the mood to face the world today. Promises made seem shallow at best. I'm feeling self-doubt, unsure about him and overall anxious about the relationship. He came back home.

Day 4--- Today there is a calm that has swept over me. A feeling of being at peace. An "Oh, there you are!" moment has taken over. I unknowingly got so wrapped up in him that I forgot who I was as an individual.

Day 5--- Today I'm embarrassed that you could just walk away. As if my feelings and emotions were expendable. Without a look back. Without a fight. Today I'm embarrassed to face the world… to face myself!

Day 6--- Today I feel like a little piece of my spirit has died. Like the zealous enthusiasm has just left the building. So this is what having the blues feels like? Today I finally get it. Reality is setting in and I finally get it. There will be no wedding. No dress. No best men and bridesmaids. No food and drink. No union. No celebration. No Mr. and Mrs. Taylor. Clarity has poisoned my vision and I suppose you can say I'm glad for it. But I must admit, I'm a bit jealous of the head over heels, blissfully, ignorant me. Unable to face reality, even though it's slapping me in the face, I've gotten rid of the dress!

Day 7--- Today makes 1 week since he crushed my happily ever after dreams. My broken heart doesn't care that spring has returned.

Spring

LOVE'S DEBT

Have you ever felt something so great had been given and you were undeserving? Well that's how I feel. I don't think I could ever match the love he has given me. Yeah, it's that monumental. I'll forever be in love's debt.

STARTING ANEW

From Square 1, Block A, the beginning, the very start. Old ghosts from a marriage past called on me, no, more like haunted me for immediate attention. It's kinda hard to plan a wedding without first having gotten divorced. The paperwork has been resubmitted, and that matter of business is in motion, now we play the waiting game... and the praying game! "I pray all is finite before..." Unable to finish the statement I feebly direct my attention on 07.30.11. Oh yeah did I mention, we finally have a venue. It's the perfect location, 5 miles from our apartment, nestled in the very city where 'we' met and 'I' fell in love; Hapeville, Georgia. The city's newly renovated historic church has been chosen as the place where he and I will exchange vows. With starch white paint, updated stained glass windows, new hardwood floors, fresh pews, visible beams at the steeple of the ceiling, and a shiny new bell. On either side of the church were gardenias and magnolias. Even the air smells pretty here. From this focal point we start anew!

FULL CIRCLE

It seems certain aspects of one's life are bound to repeat themselves. It is the way of the world and history in general. Summer vacations, barbeques, and family gatherings will never be a thing of the past... these things are as inevitable as time. However, with the change of seasons, a new perspective is born and with it history is changed and made. Graduations have commenced and my son finds himself faced with a new journey at summer's end; high school. New friends become best friends, those not blood related sometimes seem closer than kin, family dynamics change, old wounds are revealed, and temptations are denied. This thing called life really is a revolving matter. I'm learning to love...

LEMONADE

With a basket full of lemons we make lemonade. A tall glass that's both sour and sweet. The dance of life and love constantly stirring and adding new elements. Slow dancing with him is bittersweet. No matter how upset I may be, he remains my bestfriend. No need in dwelling on mistakes. All the secrets and surprises that were revealed have been laid on the table beside the spoon. They too have been stirred in. I'm not gonna take a single sip for granted. He and I together drink from this cup.

REAL ATLANTA HOUSEWIFE

No, I'm not having champagne at 7 in the morning. I don't employ any nannies, nor is there a fleet of limos parked outside my door... each with its own chauffeur. I am however drinking a glass of orange juice, which I hope does not give me heartburn. There's a stack of bills which adhere to a strict budget, a sink full of dishes, and a truck with a mind of her own. Glamorous? No. Real? Yes. Still these are the components of a real Atlanta housewife... True story.

A.T.L

Every time we go Downtown a sense of 'Wow' sweeps over me. Herman always looks over at me from the driver seat and breathes "There's your city baby." Atlanta GA, she is indeed breathtaking. I love to get caught up in the traffic wondering who each person is, what type of life they lead and where they are going. Half hanging out of the passenger seat window, adjusting the color of my digital camera to black and white. Taking mental photographs as well as digital. 4 lanes turn into 8, hov lanes, turning lanes, oncoming traffic and upcoming exits. Herman, born and raised here knows all the off the grid streets, but he knows I love the interstate. There is no better route than the scenic route. The buildings, bridges, and billboards, the latter being my favorite. I'm always intrigued by the different advertisements. I imagine there is a board of members sitting around a desk; debating, deciding the tone of the next Ad so that it will awe and amaze those traveling so to the point the next soda they drink, the next meal they consume, or the next car they drive has been influenced by one little, well one 14x48 suggestion! Herman watches me in silent adoration as I watch the city open up in front of my very eyes, each ¼ mile offering a new surprise. All the senses of this city are alive, she awakens me, and I love her and him for this gem.

WAITING

Waiting in the reception lobby of a local modeling agency for Herman, this seminar is one which could change the course of not only his life but mine as well, and I welcome whatever it entails. He has gotten so many compliments on his dashing good looks and why shouldn't he? His overall personality is beautiful, and his gorgeousness seeps out of every pore. Standing a tall 6'4", his frame lithe and long, a well-defined chiseled face, very masculine in look, style, and mannerism... he is my very own Adonis.

IN VAIN

Turns out it was a sham. One of those pay first then we'll get you work type of shams. Damn shame too. His presence really is beautiful.

TOGETHER

Our first, major pre-wedding purchase together; the most expensive set of stainless steel pots and pans. Invites were sent out to particulars via the Bridal Show that had been previously attended. A purchase wasn't necessary to win the free trip being offered just for showing up. So the Honey and I headed to Duluth. We were the first couple to arrive for the seminar. 4 other soon to be bride and grooms joined us. We sat through a thirty minute, very informative presentation, which at the end 'we' all wanted new cookware! The price was not ideal but the gifts that accompanied were. $1,000.^{00} worth of grocery coupons, a $300.^{00} gift certificate to an online jeweler, and two more all-expense paid vacations (minus travel arrangements of course, something about National Security, 9/11, and new policies). Psst, the extra vacations are what sealed the deal for Herman. I'm looking forward to relaxing on some exotic beach with him.

A NATURAL PHENOMENA

Residents of Singleville and Relationshiphood, often wonder if monogamy is a natural thing and if so, what of flirting? Are we supposed to be as horses with blinders on, never seeing what's alongside us? Only to see straight ahead? Is it wrong for individuals to want to feel desired by the opposite sex? A lingering smile, a slow hello, an extended conversation, harmless chat... what is and what is not permitted? I think I'm gonna need a Rules & Regulations handbook!

LET THEM EAT CUPCAKES

I have been informed via my sister in law to be that she is on a slow descent from cupcake heaven. Were they that divinely delicious? Eyebrows rose when I first proclaimed that the bridal cake would be no ordinary cake. Instead, I intend for our party guests to consume individual cupcakes. It's all the rave in wedding trend and you know me, forever the one breaking tradition. Ever since this proclamation has been made, she has taken it upon herself to be the royal taster. She is thoroughly enjoying this added position to her already arm length resume.

PRETTY IN FULL BLOOM

I've been noticing the flowering trees in full bloom. So pretty the white blossoms. Dogwoods. In certain areas of the city they resemble a fresh flurry. I imagine the snowcapped mountains of the Alps. Per my request Herman has intentions to pull over so that I may pluck a branch from a tree, whoa Nelly! We unexpectedly skid off the side of the road. Trailing 18 wheelers express their upset through a series of horns blowed. At first I thought Jade was up to her old tricks, not realizing his initial intent at the request of his beloved. Branch picked, back in the truck, windows up... windows down. The flowers are pretty but they've got a terrible fragrance about them. What a cruel trick of Mother Nature. Pretty only in appearance. I suppose some things are better left alone.

HIS BAD HABIT

No, he does not leave the toilet seat up nor does he forget to replace the cap of the toothpaste. He does not drink out of the orange juice carton nor does he return the ice tray to the freezer empty. Quite the gentleman he is. Why then the reoccurrence of this inconsideration? His bad habit? 1..2..3..10 steps! Ahead of me that is. This bad habit is beginning to rub me the wrong way and frankly the rubbed places have begun to chafe, flesh exposed, I'm rather raw about it.

THE ISSUE AT HAND

I've got the perfect Man, the perfect date, the perfect dress, but no site secured. This is bordering ridiculous. I'm ready to see some plans in concrete. I know that you should never write a thing down in stone because life is constantly changing. But it really is kinda hard to work towards an unseen goal. Can we at least chalk it on the sidewalk?

CUPCAKES

Who talks in the $100's when they're talking cupcakes? Well I for one think this conversation is insane. Thirty dollars for a dozen seems very, not a bit, but very steep. Deciding against the traditional wedding cake seemed like a smart decision financially speaking, not to mention what a cool idea! 150 is the agreed upon guest count, so exactly how many dozen will we need? 12 ½!!! Rounded up to 13, that's, $390, not including tax, for some cupcakes? I hate to sound frugal but cookies sure are looking scrumptious...

COMPLAINTS

You're complaining but offering very little backup. Okay, I tell the children its bedtime, they wait until I'm distracted then sneak an extra 30 minutes of television in. Instead of falling asleep, they get up for water fifty million times. And let's not speak of the revolving bathroom door. As the ages of each progress, they become less and less childlike. The waters become choppy as they navigate new territory in the quest to discover who they are. All the while testing who? You guessed it, Dear Ol' Mom! Every day is brand new to me. The art of parenting is never really mastered. We do the best we can and pray it's enough. It seems my best is sometimes not good enough for him. This is not my complaint though. The complaint is his bad judgment! Instead of voicing his feelings, thoughts, and opinions on the matter; he serves a virtual blow... via the notorious Facebook post. Hence my complaint. Why for the love of Honeybees would he go that route? It's like unfollowing the chain of command. I just don't get it. Mature enough to know a similar response is unacceptable. His reply to my refusal to respond? Taking off into the night. Great. Classic Herman. I thought we established that this was not the answer. An equal opposition however are a mother who has done the lion's share alone before the family dynamic changed and a soon to be parent whose experience with children only extend to that of his young niece and nephew. This is gonna be one hell of a storm, not all easy sailing. But we'll conquer that tempest tomorrow, for now the matter of walking out is heavy on the horizon.

HMMM

The fact that we acknowledge what we share is nowhere near perfect makes it a dysfunctional kinda love. He vents online, I complain silently, we both sulk. But when all is said and done, it's him that I lay my head and body and heart beside each night. Rome wasn't built in a day. I know we're gonna make it because I have faith that we will. Hmm. What a great thought.

STEALING SECRETS

Take, thievery? I'm no cat burglar. What I am though is a smart 'Kat', one that knows the value of borrowing ideas! Herman's sister called a meeting between an associate (who happens to be a wedding coordinator) and the soon to be married couple. A package has been proposed, a very expensive package has been proposed. But instead of freaking out over the amount of digits behind the dollar sign, I've decided to take notes. And no, I'm not stealing secrets. I'm borrowing ideas.

TOO ATTACHED

I'm pretty sure it's the onset of menopause. I mean what else could be to blame. I'm super upset today. Why? Because I've been alerted for several weeks now, that the sister in law to be prefers to spend her birthday in solitude. Odd request, but who am I not to oblige? Her birthday, her wish. So you can imagine my surprise when the Honey reports that she's having a makeshift party. Fun, food, and friends. At the mention of this I can feel the tidal wave of emotions rise up inside of me. I'm upset with her for not inviting me... I'm angry at him for telling me. Then out of those emotions come the tears. Who gave my heart permission to turn the water on? As I'm washing my tear stained face I look into the mirror. The reflection is unapologetic, mocking. "Silly girl" I sober up. I'm the oldest of my siblings, also the only girl. The Powers That Be saw fit to bless me with brothers and I'll take that. I just have to remind myself not to get too attached. She is after all 'his' sister.

DAMN, DAMN, DAMN

I've noticed a pattern with Jade. For sure she has a mind of her own and she voices her opinion often, but this opinion seems much louder on rainy days. My eldest daughter pointed it out one morning as we 'skipped' along to school, Jade threatening to have the last word. She acts up regularly but certainly when it's raining. It has me thinking. Wondering. Questioning. Is there a leak somewhere? Is the hood not sealed tight enough? Is something being flooded under there? Where's a Pep Boy when you need him? And as the thought occurs, the engine sputters off. Leaving me to sit, parked until she changes her mind. Damn, damn, damn.

GO WITH THE FLOW

It has been discovered that the life of a Bride is ever changing. Never write a single thing in stone. Colors, themes, songs, flowers, dress, location, food… the list is infinite. If it's one thing I've learned thus far it is "It's better to just go with the flow."

SPECIAL REQUEST

I'd like to request the removal of all things wedding from our cable package. The Honey is in awe of the extravagant ceremonies and receptions. The kids are even watching the bride reality shows. The house is in a pre-marital frenzy. I, the Bride, am the only calm one here? Imagine the irony of that.

BROKEN GLASS & BLOOD

... everywhere. I was super excited to show the Honey something I had been working on, so much to the point that I couldn't wait for his shower to be over. With laptop in hand, I knocked. A mishap occurred before he could undo the lock. BOOM! BANG! BAM! The loudest noise ever then not another sound. The sickest gut feeling, I knew he had fell. Seems on his way out of the shower he reaches for the towel rod, it gives under his weight, and it's "Donna, pimp down!" in my Katt Williams voice. My kitty 'Kat' voice is hysterical. Beating the paint off of the door was futile. My son ran for a knife so that I could pick or pry the lock. Nothing. Finally, I hear the knob turn and there he is in all his pride and glory, wet and disheveled. As I'm taking in the scene it looks like something out of a scary movie. Busted glass. Wet floor, but not water wet; blood wet. Drip, drip, dripping from his elbow down to the floor in the very spot I stood. Toe nails splattered red. I'm trying not to lose my mind but I can feel myself hyperventilating and I can feel the tears well up inside of me. I see the glass jutting from his elbow. Now I'm really freaking out. Frantically, I call for the tweezers, the same needle nose tweezers I used to extract the cottony doom from his ear. At least inch deep, the glass, blood trickles more profusely now. The moment is one of hysteria but his face is calm, a little too calm. Oh by the way, the pots and pans we ordered came today.

DAYDREAMING

I did it again. Got lost in my own thoughts. But every now and again a girl wants to drown out the melodramas that unfold around her. Tune into the sounds of the ocean; imagine the sun on her face, the wind at her back and the sand beneath her feet. The gentle crash at low tide. Inhale, exhale, inhale… "Awww the smell of Paradise." This beautifully remote island becomes fuzzy as I'm snatched back to the here and now. The air smells of, burning biscuits. Oh no. I did it again.

WATCHING HIM

He looks over at the window from where he lay.
Curtains drawn shut, his gaze far away.
Lids falter and threaten to shut.

Heart flutters...

I love him so much!

REALLY

It's 12:45 a.m. Monday. A new week has arrived. We should be asleep. Instead, I'm sitting at the laptop getting some patent information for Herman and he is standing in the kitchen boiling strawberries! Really? Who does that? "Baby hook it up?" no "Baby afraid, very afraid!" Will the Powers That Be protect my stomach please?

ROTATE & REVOLVE

Just as the Earth rotates on its own axis, yet revolves around the sun. So it is with the Jackson~Taylor wedding! I'm not one of those high strung brides who puts everything on hold until the big day is done. No, I continue to play this everyday game of life as it has been played all along except there is a new piece on the board. The wedding rotates on its own axis as does each component in my life. Home, children, husband to be; each in its own way revolves around me!

R & R

Rest and relaxation are in order. Herman had a great 30th birthday. With that said and done, my attention have been redirected to 07.30.11. My current but not only concern is the headcount, or er um guest list. So with a hot bath ran, the list in hand, and the Black Eyed Peas at repeat, I write and rewrite until the list is finite.

COULD IT BE

A location to exchange vows, say I do and pledge eternal love to each other! Could it be? A call from the bestie has me in an extremely optimistic mood. Me happy? You bet... and I should be!

-50

The engagement party turnout was ½ the invite list. And despite the great time we had, only his sister and her family showed up for his 30th Birthday Celebration; the wedding list which has been whittled down to 150 is being examined and re-determined. Those that have been there from day 1 thereafter have priority. What this means is this one simple thing... my cousin's neighbor's sister in law's best friend's daughter Tracy will not be in attendance. Those at the core of our lives, within our circle... Those that have provided a great example and given unending support in our union have what I deem, 'Seniority'.

HOW TO BECOME A BRIDE

(OR GROOM):

CREATING THE PERFECT GUEST LIST

No, Tracy does not make the first 50 cut. She does not make the first 100 cut either. There are so many, too many templates to choose from when compiling this elite list. Adding to the ever growing stack of 'Bride's things to do list...' I've found it best to do whatever works for you. Although the approach I use is rather untraditional, as if! When I think of those closest to us, I can mentally 'see' a circle where they reside at our core. Then I can see the ripples and reflections of the bordering circles. Ever seen a Nesting Doll? This is the effect I imagine and it's the technique I use to create the perfect guest list. With this in mind the idea for an easy template comes to mind, The Spider's Web. Placing at the center; parents, siblings, grandparents, and children... webbing out to aunts, uncles, first cousins and their immediate families... further webbing out to the bridal party, their children and spouses... continued webbing beyond this includes friends, classmates, coworkers and last but not least those elusive extended family members. You can add as many or as few elements of The Spider's Web as you deem necessary, the church and reception hall is close to capacity, or budget does not allow... Or the rule I prefer: The smaller the Web, the more Intimate the wedding. But like I stated before, whatever works for you! G'luck and happy planning!

PSST, SECRET FITTING

I know, I know, I said I was done looking and I was... in person. But that never stopped me from internet window shopping. A few emails from my chosen bridal boutique has finally enticed me to go for that secret fitting. Having made the mistake of having Herman with me at the first two fittings, 'bad idea' one consultant chided. Two more fittings consisted of the company and very opinionated voice of my sister in law to be. They say the 3rd time's a charm, I was hoping the same holds true for the 5th. Herman insisted I go out, take a moment for myself and indulge in that oh so secret fitting. I'm glad I did.

DRESS #5

Not 1, 2, 3, or 4 but 5. The secret fitting went great. I had a distinct idea of an even better dress. Not that 'the one' previously chosen was less than, but the vision of this one was better. In my arsenal of preparedness were the date, time, and location. With these things in mind I was ready to make my final decision. I even took the shoes with me so that I could get an overall feel... and it was magical! Perfect shoes meet perfect dress. Perfect dress meet perfect me. Hello dress #5!!! I can't wait for Herman to see me in it. After 40 days of no in-depth physical contact, him seeing me in this dress, I'm sure to get a full salute...

LAST NAME DENOUNCED

An irritating little beast has reared its ugly head. I never thought much on the topic before but here I am, contemplating the last name change. I know it's customary for girls to take their father's last name at birth and the last name of her husband's father at the time of marriage. But here is where the plot thickens. My parents were born and raised during a very odd time, the 60's. Everyone was wearing tie dyed shirts, bell bottom jeans, and platform shoes. They were seriously sticking it to 'the man' and evidently all that flower power didn't plant many marriages. This seed is not bitter in the least. I was raised by the better half of the once upon a time duo, my mother. Hence my last name was her last name for a very long time. Then several years later and a legal matter too, my last name became that of my estranged father. And despite the non-relationship I have with him I wear the name proudly. It is after all my grandfather's name. It's the last thing aside from memories that I have of *him*. Jackson. Given to me around the age of 11, I've lived with it for the past 20 years. Needless to say, I'm rather attached! This brings me back to the matter at hand. To change or not to change, that is the question. Herman does not want me to denounce my last name! He has suggested that I simply add to. No hyphen or weird accent but one name altogether, that which my mother, my grandfather and now he have blessed me with. Katandra Shanel Jackson Taylor, I can dig it. Solid.

KATANDRA VON TAYLOR

Sometimes I feel like I was born beyond my time. That déjà vu feeling of been here done that is always near. I have been looking into some retro wedding ideas and I'd love to incorporate a few of those elements. This played part in my dress selection. The lace overlay has a very vintage feel. I'm fascinated with the hairstyles of years gone. Thinking of deep finger waves with flower clips. A local stylist has revealed this hairstyle to be her specialty, but she refers to them as 'ocean waves'. I've also inquired about the process to dye my hair siren red. I need to start toying with ideas now so that when the big day comes I will be perfectly coifed.

MUM'S THE WORD

With unfinished business looming ever so ominously overhead, talk of wedding bells have screeched to a silence. It's just impossible to plan a happy future with the ugly past slapping you in the face. The big day is fast approaching, the days are narrowing, and even though my face remains calm underneath the silence, I'm actually in quite the traumatic state.

PUSHING AGAINST A DEADLINE

It is exactly that. 56 days left until I become Mrs. Taylor, no more soon to be. With each passing day I'm reminded of the urgent matter at hand. The, dare I say it, "Divorce!" I now have less time to wrap up unfinished business. Not to mention the 31 day waiting period before trial. Yep, I'm officially insane. And as if this wasn't enough to deal with. I complicated it in a beautiful way, the wedding party.

HONORARY CHICA

Guess who done went and did it again? Me? How'd you know? What gave me away? I've added 1 more to the bride's side of the wedding party; a much unexpected acquaintance turned Ace. The closer she and I became, I knew without a doubt that my day would not be as special if she were merely an onlooker. So with a push from my Honey, another insane moment has spurred of this thought. I've asked this amazing friend if she would take part in my special day. With only weeks left and wedding talk on mute; minor and major details must be decided, a dress needs to purchased, a requested leave of absence via work; so much for a bridesmaid (I mean Mejor Chica) to accomplish in just a few weeks. The question asked. The answer, YES! No hesitation, no doubts, simply yes. On such short notice, I consider her my Honorary Chica. She's proving to be more than a friend and Herman is glad to have her on board. She is a part of our circle now. My Honorary Chica.

MINOR DETAILS DECIDED

+ 1 has proven to be quite the lucky number. Immediately she has gone into super help mode. So is that what traditional bridesmaid types do? Hmmm. Wonders and just as quickly walks away from that idea. You know me, running from tradition and tweaking each detail I can to make it all mine. Slowly, minor details are being decided. It's about time.

LADY IN WAITING

My lackluster locks are a direct result of too much hair dye and too many perms. Nobody ever told me too much of a good thing ain't exactly a good thing. My misguided knowledge has had an anything but positive end result; to say the least and spare particulars "I look like a shaggy dog!" No exaggeration here. I so want to cut, chop, clip it back to its healthy state; you know, in short, make the nightmare go away! But Herman has ever so graciously asked that I wait until after the wedding. Talk about Karma.

MANIC BRIDE

I've committed myself to some insane get healthy get fit quick tricks. There was the skip breakfast and lunch diet but all that did was encourage overeating during dinner. Then there was the lemon juice mixed with water, cayenne pepper and maple syrup diet supplement which was supposed to be a substitute for food altogether. The only downfall with this one was that the very taste before full consumption was enough to trigger my psychological gag reflexes and by day 3, I was starving. I tried the all fruit and veggie/no bread diet, the no sugar diet, the child's portion diet; these in addition to the exercise until I hurt plan. My response to each? No, nope, no thanks, no way... N-O! My Honey suggested I work out and eat in moderation. Not a child's portion per se but enough to satiate and a workout plan he himself designed; earning him the title 'Malicious One'. Up the stairs, down the stairs, up the stairs, down the stairs, up the stairs, down the stairs, up the... I think you get the point. This repeated calorie burning, thigh toning, butt firming workout in repetitions of 12 multiplied by 2 flights of stairs, each set of 4 count as 1. That's a total of............48 flights? Hmph. Then he has the mercy to let me walk reps 6 and 12, but the remainder is done at a steady sprint. Afterwards I grab a quick drink of h2o and grab a spot on the living room floor for a set of 50 sit-ups! It's been hard work but I just know my wedding dress is gonna thank me.

BETTER THAN THE BEST

Before laying his head down to sleep, he remembers me. Such a shock to see my satin scarf at my pillow. No frantic search tonight. Instead, a wave of terror has washed over me. How could my heart go on if something should happen to him? What if he got sick or had an accident. I'd like to report I was able to dismiss this thought but that would be a lie. So I've adopted a parallel realization. He's better than the best and I've been divinely blessed; if not for an eternity, at least in this lifetime. My fears have been caressed by this revelation, momentarily.

DEUCES? NO, ACES!

Since Chica numero 4 has joined the wedding family, my life has been made a Bridal Bliss. It's not that diamonds and pearls have unexplainably and inexplicably shown up on my threshold; no, nothing of the sort. And it's not that she is so very different from the others, but then again, she is... they all are. In some weird way that I can't quite seem to put into words, they mirror pieces of me; my Bestie, my PIC (partner in crime), of course my Bridesmaidzilla, and now my Ace. They complement and complete me in a way that only sisters can. I suppose it really is okay that female siblings were not born unto me because these ladies really do take the cake.

Summer

A CHANGE OF PLANS

The days are winding down and the date is getting closer. Unfinished business stills looms in the air. The stench is growing ever near and the pungency is making me sick. If all is not wrapped up by July 1st, our date will be pushed back... again. Sometimes it feels like the day is never gonna come to pass and that I will never have the honor of calling myself his wife. This feeling hurts. I maintain my sanity as I think of the pretty summer time wedding dress and the 'before' winter colors of my wedding party. No need to alarm the guest since invitations have not been decided upon let alone sent out. A change of plans may be in order, an alternate date is being considered; a possible fall wedding may be in the works. Talking with one of las chicas, my PIC to be exact, has revealed a delicious idea. It would be very cool to have a Halloween type party or a masquerade if you will. Then it dawned on me, how beautifully wicked would it be to have a masquerade themed wedding. She has decided to come dressed as a Prom Queen from the Dead. Creepy. The result of too many criminal investigation and forensicy television programs I'm certain. We've already spotted the perfect place to get 'costumes' from. Now to run the idea by Herman, but this won't be immediately. Didn't I mention my 3 week vacation? La chica is at the wheel and I am en route to Manassas Georgia. What was I writing about before I rambled off? Oh yeah... a Masquerade Wedding! If July 30th should come and wedding bells don't ring. I won't be sad. I've got the rest of my life to spend with him, and I intend for it to be a Ball!

LOVE BRINGS CHANGE AND CHANGE BRINGS PATIENCE… HOPEFULLY

I don't believe it has come as much of a surprise to our impending guests that the date has been rescheduled yet again. Many eyebrows have risen just the same though, on the faces of each except for a great aunt. She has calmly brought back into focus the priority of USSR Jackson~Taylor. And that focus is to build a strong, solid, steadfast foundation on which Happily Ever After will survive. Her words, "What's the hurry? If this is going to be the last go around, take your time." And I intend to. Herman has taught me that love brings change and change brings a patience even we are unaware of. I'm glad in his aura as I wait in love.

MAKESHIFT PILLOWCASE

It's official. I'm really missing him tonight. I'm glad to be visiting my parents and cutting in on the kids summer vacation, but so much time away from him is heart wrenching. It's downright sad if you ask me. The tee he slept in the night before my departure had been vacuum sealed in a bag to retain its freshness, and it was kinda like I forgot about it but not really. As the memory of its whereabouts flood my memory, I dig frantically for it. Upon retrieval I press the cold, scented cotton tee to my face and I-N-H-A-L-E. His kisses and caresses tease my senses. And as my lungs fill of him I count down the days until my return. I strip my bedmate of its suddenly not good enough pillowcase and drape his tee over the lump instead. Hugged close to my chest... I miss him.

TEMPTATION

Sometimes the grass really is greener on the other side. But the manure that lay beneath the lush mirage is so not worth the trouble. Even with this knowledge a formidable weapon in my arsenal, temptation still comes a 'knockin. Sometimes the knock is so subtle that it falls upon deaf ears. But other times the rapping is deafening and a once indulging soul is forced to conjure up willpower and determination. This vacation just got longer. By the way did I mention I'm really missing my Honey and his sweet as nectar kisses?

MAYBE THERE'S HOPE YET

A bride to be may have hinted once or twice via two mutually single friends, how amazing it would be for their oneness to come together. Strictly an internet relationship, finally numbers exchanged. I've heard tale of their voice communication. Maybe there's hope yet. But then again, with all this business of temptation, I'm not so sure la 'single' chica should complicate her life with the jigsaw of love. All the wondering is enough to drive a well-meaning friend insane.

BLING, BLING, BLING PART 4

SAYING GOODBYE TO THE RING

The plastic adjuster that came compliment of a too big ring lost its firm grip weeks ago. I've even had dreams of losing the ring because of its looseness. Then there was the dream where I was taking out the garbage and the ring slipped right off of my hand into the trash receptacle. And another one in which I'm washing my hands and the ring washes down the drain, never to be retrieved. Shakes the daymare from the forefront of my mind, where was I? Oh yeah, saying goodbye to the ring. Herman instructed that I leave the bling behind before I embarked for my summer escapade so that he could have it resized... again. In my despair, I requested a loaner! Isn't that what they do? Give you a 'not as fabulous' automobile while yours is away for repairs... isn't this the same thing?

NERVOUS KAT IN THE WILD

The water pressure way too low in the guest bathroom, I decide to jump in my parent's shower. Well, jump is not quite the enthusiastic verb I'd like to use. Nervously treaded comes to mind. I didn't always feel this way.

Flashback.

It all began on a hot summer day several years ago. It was the kinda hot that breaks weather records. The heat index was surely off the charts! I was home alone. Not forced to shower in my parent's bathroom, but opting to. That new shower head really did optimize the water pressure which was already great back there, I think we all secretly loathed the guest bathroom for this very reason. So with hair pulled high into a ponytail, the towel draping my body, I commenced to 'jump' in the shower. At their bedroom doorway I stop. I forgot my clothes, so I backtrack to retrieve them. In their bedroom near my mother's vanity mirror, a belt lay on the floor. Before I could pick it up, it moves... an ever so slight slither. I slowly back away. Hoping my sin-glasses eyes are playing tricks on me. But they aren't. So clearly, if my eyes are not deceiving me, then my mind must be. With glasses on I return to the room once more only to find that the 'belt' is gone. Now I'm worried. Frantically and hesitantly I scanned the perimeter of the garden style bath. I see a tail disappear under the bathroom door. I jam a towel underneath, dress, run outside... not a car in sight. Phone in hand, numbers dialed... not an answer. It was up to me to handle the situation until help arrived. The bathroom door creaked open at my beckon. Stepping back, I scan the room from a safe distance. In the corners, behind the toilet, on the floor; no snake! Just then I hear the Calvary arrive. I explain the scene to my parents. My step father retrieves a shovel. Again, we search the bathroom; still no snake. Then I open the frosted glass door of the shower thinking, 'There is no way he could he could have gotten in here.' The floor of the shower is bare. My step father and I look at each other quite perplexed. Just then we hear an ever so light scraping sound overhead... THE SNAKE!!! I have to be honest here. I've been a little weary of the lou ever since. Nervous at best.

SUBCONSCIOUS MOCKINGS

My hand is inside of a clear bag. My bling upon the ring finger of her owner. I turned my hand toward the sun to induce a shine so bright, even the stars would weep in obvious envy. But instead of glitz and glimmer I got nothing. An empty setting. I inspect the bag for the dislodged diamond and discover two instead of one. I open the bag picking the diamonds up. In a desperate panic I try to mount them in the empty setting, one and then the other. Nothing! Neither of them fit, leaving the frightful emptiness there to haunt me. Why... why... why? Pithful mutterings. Then I awake. What had the dream meant? What had I done to cause such a disturbance to result in a dislodged diamond? And why were there 2 diamonds loose in the bag? Perhaps I banged my hand against something causing the gem to be 'free'! But that still doesn't explain where the extra diamond came from. Could one mistake lead to the loss of two? This question has left me with one conclusion...

... the subconscious underlyings of temptations in my dreams have come to mock me.

COUNTRY BRIDE... CITY FEET

Could it be? My southern culture is being taken over by city ways? Herman is always getting onto me! "Baby put on some shoes, Atlanta isn't Manassas!" I grudgingly oblige. Too much pampering of one's feet is not a good thing. I'm rather upset at the once familiar now foreign feel of white sand, red clay, and jagged pebbles sifting through forgetful toes... Oh how they used to remember. For once since my uprooting and replanting in Atlanta, I've grown frustrated with the city I love and now call home for domesticating me. Imagine that; A country bride with city feet. Whoever heard of such a thing?

ABSENCE MAKES THE HEART GROW FONDER

They say absence makes the heart grow fonder. Well, fonder or not, one thing it certainly has provoked are quite a few memories. This 'vacation' away from him has gone on long enough. Not to mention, everything reminds me of his face, his smell, his touch, his embrace, his kisses. Damned q-tips. How could something as simple as inspecting the household essential for quality not quantity has me remembering the time he got that fluffy white cloud of doom & disaster stuck in his ear. I can laugh about it now, but it was not funny in the moment. What is was though however was the first mishap I endured at the hands of being in love with him. Was I gonna be able to get it out? Would surgery be required to extract something so seemingly harmless? Would he lose the hearing in that ear? With luck and a trip to the local pharmacy for a pair of needle nose tweezers, I Nurse Betty'd the puffy cloud of shame from his ear canal. He asked me to never speak of it, so mums the word between these pages, okay? By the way did I mention that he's quite the artist? Picasso in fact. A pan of hot grease, a few burgers, a spatula, and an unskilled hand and walah! A very painful masterpiece. But that's another entry entirely!

MISSING HIS KISSES

Week two has commenced and last night was the worst. Not even a phone call. My hands have been very busy with the children and I know he's been hard at work. Still this is the first time I've been away from him for more than 2 days since moving into our apartment together last summer, and I've gotta admit, I could never be a military wife! I'm literally counting the hours.

Today has made the 10th day without his touch, without his kisses. I'm literally driving myself insane. In my temporary madness I recall an article I once read; something to the effect of '40 days with/40 days without'. The read was interesting but I've come to realize I could never be the victor of such a challenge in his presence. Now that I think of it, Herman wasn't too thrilled about the proposal of 40 days with and 40 days without sexual contact, even though intimate closeness is allowed. However, the 40 days with *'did'* peak more than his interest. But who am I kidding? I'm missing him like crazy and it's only been a few days... do cold showers work for girls too?

BEFORE MY ♥ FOR HIM THERE WAS ANOTHER

Childhood memories are like the ancient wonders of the world; few, precious, and scattered. Being in this house away from Herman and my wife-to-be duties has yielded some very remarkable memories. One of my fondest is recalling my infinite love of books. I would marvel at their inviting covers remembering not to judge too deeply the surface. I would thoroughly inspect pages, thumbing in a fan like motion so that the familiar scent of 'Once Upon A Time' would fill my nostrils, taking special care to note Author, Copyright date, and Publisher. I've always been intrigued by the Special Thanks and Acknowledgements, I suppose it's because I have a special affinity for those that love and support me to no end. I would sit up all night against my mother's will; her argument would always be an impedingly daunting electric bill. But even amidst her admonishing, she never left me in the dark. All those nights snuggled up against pillows, dolls, and teddy bears. Ever so close to the light of the lamp, always reading "just one more paragraph… just one more page… just one more chapter" But the end of one chapter always spilled over onto another. Me and books had a love/hate relationship. I loved to read well into a new day, unable to close the great novel at my fingertips. Transferring me to a parallel universe, transforming my thoughts, feelings, and emotions; I'd be in a zombie-like trance from beginning to bittersweet end. I always hated the last chapter, that last page; that dreaded last paragraph. I'd always be enthralled by the H.E.A (Happily Ever After) but not so thrilled about 'The End'. It has dawned on me, this recollection, that even before my first diary was given to me I had fallen in love with the written word. We still have a love/hate relationship and Mr. Taylor never dissuades the affair. In fact he encourages it.

BUTTERFLIES ARE BAD

Contrary to popular belief, butterflies are indeed *'The'* menace to society. They are not these beautiful gilded insects that reflect signs of spring. No, what they are though is quite the opposite. If you could imagine for a moment... the feel of cold steel against your skin; imagine that sick gut feeling you conjure at the anticipated pain of an unforgiving blade; digging, twisting, ripping away at flesh. The moment right before evil impales—Butterflies! I don't know who coined the term but it's true. You can really feel the anxiety fluttering about. It's that feeling you get when you are about to do something terribly wrong. A dear cousin has asked if this feeling had begun to occur within me. A slight pause revealed an easy answer... No! In my opinion, brides who get butterflies are somewhere deep down having doubts. I view this dreaded sensation as a sign of uneasiness, insecurity, and apprehension. If a girl is feeling those things in regards to one of the biggest decisions of her life, then perhaps marriage should wait and in its place a spa day should be scheduled, that's sure to invoke a serene calm.

<u>NOTHING, I REPEAT NOTHING, IS EVER GONNA BE PERFECT</u>

A light rapping at the door, "Come in" the distinguished voice called from the other side. Behind the desk looking very much in his element, glasses upon his face, more salt than pepper in his hair, his smile genuine and welcoming… priceless; the father of my ex. At my grand entrance his eyes twinkled, clearly glad to see me, either that or grateful for the interruption. We talked, we laughed, we reminisced; it was great to see him! He gave me two pieces of very important advice: 1) "Don't let nothing or nobody steal you away. Remember where you come from. Remember where home is." & 2) "Nothing is ever perfect. Sometimes you have to jump right in!" After saying our goodbyes I called my Honey. "I love you. I wanna marry you. Nothing is ever gonna be perfect." I smile because he "…knows…" Could it be? Are we in premarital, blissful agreeance? I'm enjoying this 'perfect' moment.

MURDER SHE WROTE

The summer months always put me on edge. The heat induced hysteria never fails and I automatically reach for the scissors. Yes, I'm the one who asked the Taylor wedding party not to make any more drastic changes via their tresses; especially Las Mejor Chicas. But as the summer solstice neared I confess that I was dying to cut my hair. I'm not talking a healthy trim, I'm talking chop... super short; but he loves my past shoulder length black, brown, auburn red hair. Loves to wrap his hands up in the freshly permed silkiness when he kisses me. But I'm beyond delusional in his absence. The only cure? A few quick snips and I'm healed. Looking in the sink at 'his' beloved hair, the very hair he asked me not to cut until after the wedding, the very wedding that has been pushed back, again. I hope I haven't just written the prescription for my demise. I'm certain he'll love me in the morning; long hair or short.

2 A.M WAKEUP

I did my best to wait up for him but I failed miserably. The nights of staying up late, lost in another world, reading and writing had finally caught up to me and I was catching some much needed zzzz's! I don't know if he attempted to rouse me or if it was his presence that shook my soul. Eyes blinked delusionally. The brink of sleep state and reality blurred everything around me. Then focus. And there he was. Like some dream come true, he was there. 2 A.M. Late. Tired. But Glad. My summer vacation had reached its end.

WHAT GREEN THUMB?

I'm very envious of anyone that has ever grown anything. The vegetable garden my ex in laws keep, the near death plants given to my mother because she has the gift of 'plant revival', the emerald green thumb of a very dear friend. I on the other hand have the uncanny ability to kill bamboo and cacti. I'm afraid to breathe in the presence of intentional lush. I don't want to kill anything with my brown thumb vibe. Why then after seeing the complete horror in my eyes have I been given two pepper plants to care for? A scotch bonnet and a habanero; I'm mortified despite the noble intent. The beautiful, green, alive plants were selected carefully and entrusted to of all people, me. I've been given good advice by their previous owner, on how to not kill them before returning to Atlanta and of their aftercare beyond the arrival at their new home. My mother suggested I give them names, but not just any ol' names, women names. So I've named one after her since it was her suggestion, and I named the other after a grandmother memory won't allow me to recall. I suppose I'll do my best not to kill them. That would be a tragedy. Hang on ladies, it's gonna be a bumpy ride!

I CALL HIM 'HONEY'

Such an endearing term, I know! Kinda girly you say? Hmph... I beg to differ. I call him Honey because his love is the sweetest nectar my tongue has ever known. The mere hint of his lovin' instills a rush that I'm certain only sugar in its purest form could conjure. I'm drawn to him. Like moth to flame so is Bee to Honey. Hence the sappy term of endearment. I think it's cute and he never complains, just keeps giving me that sweeter than sugar lovin'. I call him Honey because he is...

SUBMISSION & COMMONALITY

The how to stay happily married for 30+ years advice is not an easy pill to swallow. The "Have something in common" part is easy enough, but the 'submission' part.!? That could be a bit challenging. A conversation with a cousin as well as the talk I had with La Chica's mother have not been taken lightly. But it's easier said than done as are most things. I've gotten so used to being the strong, independent, head of household type... that's what being a single mother gets ya. But it's not going to get me far in marital bliss. Trial and error. A conversation has been brought to me by my husband to be. Now usually I go off on the deep end. Get all self-righteous just to get my point across. But this 'great' advice is humming in my head, so instead of some snazzy reply I darn near bite my tongue off. But I know as soon as he stops talking, it's full speed ahead... a piece of my mind. After the conversation ends and the smoke settles, I present Herman with this unsettling image of submission I've conjured from none other than this business of commonality and *submission.* Then one more piece of advice. He suggests that we just listen when the other talks no matter how heated the matter at hand may get. I've decided to swallow without pride, this spoonful of advice.

PARANOIA BUG

There's just something about being lied to, cheated on and done real wrong, that eats at whatever subliminal bliss that dares to linger. Taking tiny bites as not to alarm you that your trust is in danger until it's too late. By that time there's a hole the size of the Grand Canyon. And what should creep in to fill that void? None other than the ol' paranoia bug. Penetrating from within, workings its way out; infecting the mind so that every thought seems conspired. A mutiny has raged war at the home front within my internal self. Heart wants to believe, but mind has been tricked; deceived.

Checking closets, pillows, cabinets... his 6th sense must have alerted him of my distraught mood. Standing toe to toe with him, his hands firmly upon my shoulders he laid worries to rest. The past and the hurt associated with it are behind me. Funny, I didn't believe so until this moment. Honestly I didn't know I was still holding on to it. Herman assures me of my place. I guess sometimes you gotta be bitten to prompt a reminder.

HOW TO BECOME A BRIDE (OR GROOM): HAVE A PLAN

If you've met the guy (or gal) of your dreams and you can't fathom losing him (or her) before the two of you have officially become an item... you must have a plan! As an easy to follow analogy, I refer to shopping. Say you've spotted an amazing steal on the perfect beach wear but it's the middle of winter and you've put on a few pounds. Do you walk away from a great deal or do you make the purchase and make a plan to eat right and shed that winter weight? Case in point being, you must have a plan. Necessary steps and procedures are unique to each situation, but know that without a plan, you're likely to reach wedded bliss... NEVER!

RISE & FALL

Just as the sun rises and falls each day, so did July 31st. The day came so quietly and unexpectedly that half the morning had passed before I realized, 'In a few short hours, I should be Mrs. H. L. Taylor II.' But instead of walking down the aisle, we (our children +1, my niece) are en route to claim a kid friendly Saturday outing. Not the way I thought this day would unfold several months ago, but a day in his life is worth more than an eternity without him. I suppose I can conquer that galaxy another day. Just as my Aunt pointed out in a most indirect way... the rights to the kingdom are mine. What's the hurry? I'll enjoy the frills of being his Queen when that time arrives; today I'm just happy to be his Princess.

PARALLEL UNIVERSE

In this great big world, I've discovered many galaxies and amongst them, universes. Most existing alone (birthing a child, overcoming a fear, the life of a writer). Sure there are others around to witness these events, but it is the act, that must be accomplished alone. Still those worlds that coexist are just as special. Upon entering this new season I've acquired a new universe, a parallel universe! Not only am I a bride to be, I'm also the mother of a teen. Ouch! I know. Girls and hormones, games and hormones, backtalk and hormones, changes I as a previously single mother am not quite ready to encounter, and oh yeah did I mention hormones?! My son couldn't have chosen a better time to exit the caterpillar. It's shaping up to be a slow, agonizing metamorphosis. His transition to become a man and mine to become a bride has been anything but painless thus far. I wish that I could report different but that would be quite the lie. As with most rewards in life, these things too come with a price and has its moments of ups and downs. All we can do is hope that the ups far outweigh the downs thus making it worth the journey.

MY FAVORITE PART OF THE DAY IS...

...when he walks through the door after a long, hard 12+ hours at work. This life we have ain't one of glitz and glam. And yes, he gives his all the better part of each day in a much appreciated effort to provide that which we need. And no, not every want is tended. But I am fully aware of the desire he has to fulfill all things. It's because of this I stop what I'm doing to unlace steel toed boots, wrestle to pull them off of tired feet and unroll wet, sweaty, stinky socks. Ewww. But this is the part of the day I most look forward to because in his own way he does the same thing for me.

CONTRARY TO POPULAR BELIEF

I thought guys liked it when girls made an attempt to understand that which eludes most by nature. Hey I can't help it if I was given dolls instead of balls and bats. So in my understated misunderstanding I've unknowingly treaded on sacred territory. The trance like stare in his eyes should have warned me, but nooooooooo! I just had to ask some simple question that I'm sure he would have gladly elaborated on any other day. His response? "Go on now, don't be in here trying to talk football with me!!" Harsh. Well excuse me for trying to add to the list of commonalities.

DENIAL. IT REALLY IS A RIVER

Denial really is a river of endless flowing shame and guilt. He came in, changed out of his work clothes, kissed me hello and goodbye (same kiss) and he was gone. How befitting, a casting call he attended several weeks ago. Even if he doesn't get a call back it's okay. He's the leading man in my life and he always plays the role of supporting friend. So it's no surprise when he decides to spend time outside of home with an ex coworker. Thing is, I had just finished my first glass of wine when he made the announcement. Is it my fault that I had disposed of an entire bottle upon his return? Had he been home I never would have drank so much.

THE FUN ONE

"When's Herm Herm coming home? What time does he get off? Will he play the game with me once he's here? Where is he taking us this weekend? Why is Herm Herm running late from work?"

Um, no, this is not me, but the voice of 3 chickadees. I do believe they're smitten with their soon to be stepfather. And nothing warms my heart more, but I must admit, it sucks not being 'the fun one'. It seems my beloved has fallen into the traditional role of 'Dad'!

Fall

A TITLE WITHIN A TITLE:

RANDOM THOUGHTS & THE RETURN OF BRIDESMAIDZILLA

Someone suggested we jump the broom. Somebody offered up their congratulations on the elopement. Someone warned me that family can be very strange. Something or another was mentioned about a conflicting date. That last thought is actually what spurred my current mood and a slew of random thoughts. The Return of Bridesmaidzilla in all her guts and glamorous glory. My mind's eye has captured her as 'Forever the Divasaurus'. It seems the date we have rescheduled our wedding for, just so happens to be her birthday; purely coincidental. I mean forgive me for the unintentional insensitivity, but I'm not exactly sitting in my office coordinating my big day around dates of those preoccupied on the calendar. If I take this approach, Herman and I won't ever get married. It's a fact that despite the day we marry, someone somewhere will no doubt share our day. Doesn't that just make it more special?

A PASSING THOUGHT

My most favorite thing about the 'bling' is the unmistakable tan line around my ring finger. It's a sure fire sign a woman is taken.

2 A.M... AT IT AGAIN

The fiancé is fast asleep, drooling all over my pillow, funny how that happens every night. The kids have finally stopped moving and their breathing has broken even. And I am once again, at peace. This is the only time I can come undone. So what if I'm delirious beyond belief when the sun rears its beautiful head. Never mind if I'm a tad cranky when it's time to set the family in motion again. Who cares if I'm sleep deprived and that I'd probably bleed Folgers if I cut myself on the corner of the desk when I fall asleep and topple out of my 'not so' comfy office seat. All I know is that this is my time and I rather relish it.

BREAKING TRADITION

Something borrowed, something blue... Something old, something new... A silver six-pence in her shoe? Okay, so when did that saying change? Or is it that this is the way it was intended and we are the ones that altered it? It's no doubt with so many different couples making that sacrificial leap of faith that tradition is tried, true, tested and then broken! That last part is where I come in. If it's against the grain, I'm all for it! So why then is this tradition so important? Let's see; because I really want to incorporate something 'old' into my 'new' day. One 'old' thing of particular interest to me belongs to the one grandparent my memory won't allow me to recollect, my mother's mother! I found the heirloom when I was a young girl. Digging through Niecy's jewelry box was and still is a favorite past time. I love to see how alike we are and how unique she is. The jewelry box has changed throughout the years, but the one constant that remains the same is my Grandmother's watch. A brass toned metal band with an oval, pearl like face. I dunno about the other somethings and I certainly haven't a clue as to where I can acquire a silver six-pence. But one thing I'm certain of is that my grandmother's watch will be on my person when it's time for me to make that sacrificial leap of faith, for the last time.

NAKED

I've just been informed by my dear husband to be, and I quote "I'm not wearing any panties!" I'm literally laughing out loud. Out of nowhere in the midst of nothing, he appears to make this announcement. My response, "It's okay; I'm not wearing any boxers!" I've officially been reduced to a giggling fit of tears. He's not just handsome, he's hilarious!

2 ½ SUGARS, 3 CREAMS

Just as you're getting comfy in love, transformations begin to take place. Needless to say, the subtlety of each makes them hard to watch as they transpire. Still, when change occurs and its evolution is complete, only a fool doesn't see. But not I! I'm appreciative and aware. However this does not stifle my surprise when he appears before me, my favorite coffee mug in hand. "2 ½ sugars, 3 creams." he states and I'm dumbfounded! I had no idea he'd been watching as I go about my days and fulfill the little needs. It's these small deeds that have built him up to a gargantuan status in my heart. I have this overwhelming sense of being full. I think I just fell in love all over again.

P.S Did I mention his efforts to make shorter strides? Of course I would miss that transformation, but I'm glad for the change; my short legs are grateful as well!

MEAT CAKE

Really needing to speak to my mother but unable to at the moment, I turn to Google in search of an easy meat loaf recipe. Herman has agreed to cook dinner with me tonight. I'm preparing chicken to fry and he is gathering all things meat loaf. All ingredients put in, mixed up, oven on. I specifically recall asking him to shape the meat in the form of a loaf, instead he flattened it. Peeking in I discover the meat cake baking!

DRUNKEN KISSES

His kisses are intoxicating. Well they are suffocating that's for sure. Whenever lips meet, somehow we seem to meld as one. This is not advised for the respiratory system. Him suffocating me and me suffocating him, literally smothering each other in kisses. The lack of air tends to leave me a little woozy.

POSSESSED? PERHAPS!

I've been asked on several occasions, what has possessed me to keep a diary (or journal if you will) at such a busy time in one's life. Wedding planning, dealing with unexpected delays, struggling through the throes of teenagehood (AGAIN! HELP!)... add to this the equation of a normal routine! Asked again, who in their right mind actually has time? The answer to that very logical question is simple... No one! But I've made it my mission to keep a record of every recollection I can recall in hopes that one day I'll look back and say "Whoa, what a crazy line to get on this roller coaster ride. I'd do it again in a fraction of a heartbeat."

PRIME CONDITIONS

They say, "If you build it, they will come…" I don't know who 'they' are, but apply this theory loosely to matters of the heart. If you build a right mind, one that is open and forgiving then your heart will follow and become more accepting! When conditions are prime, love will come. It took me quite some time to realize this. It seems my rainy season is coming to an end. I'm ready to begin again.

CAPTAIN OR CO-PILOT

Single women often complain that they want a man, but boast that they don't need a man! I can point the finger because I've been this woman. A marriage is a union in which two individuals coexist. Coincidence? I think not. I need him to pump the gas, put air in the tire, check the oil, change the printer cartridge, figure out the remote's control, hook up the dvd player, reach the platter on the tallest shelf, change the light bulb, take out the trash... the list is infinite and ever changing. I must admit, yes, I can do these things myself. But that is not the point. The point is this; not only do I want him in my life, I need him as well. What good is a man that has no purpose? That reminds me, "Honey...!?"

HE'S A KEEPER

He still makes reservations, opens and holds doors, pulls out seats, allows me to order first, leads grace before we eat. He takes to heart when something bothers me and he goes to great lengths to correct any faults. He has the courage and the wisdom to voice his opinion and to let me know when I may be the one at fault. He not only remembers me, he considers me and I just know beyond a shadow of a doubt, beyond my own heart's beat that he is a keeper.

REARRANGING THE LIVING ROOM

For the past few weeks now, his brother-in-law has been trading kids with the Honey and I. Every other weekend my niece visits us or our children are transported there. It's a welcome break. The first thing we do after doing the happy dance is rearrange the living room. Love seat and sofa are made to meet at an angle and the top mattress of our queen size bed is relocated. From there we commence to have a kid free weekend. I love this time spent with him.

LOVE AIN'T PERFECT

I pray to the Powers that Be… may the words that I have recorded here be a reminder to me that love ain't perfect. Yes, we have more good days than bad, and I can see how from the outside looking in, our coziness seems grande. But this, it, our love is an ever evolving work in progress. By no means are he and I the exception, but we certainly are the rule. And when it comes to love, there are none.

I RESIGN

The thing with love is this... It doesn't matter how much the feeling, the emotion, the sentiment is reciprocated; it's fruitless unless it's appreciated. I've got no 'fall in love' fairy dust or songs of sirens or arrows borrowed from Eros. And although my methods, techniques, and psychological perception have been likened to the hammer of common sense, my powers of persuasion can't make anyone fall in love. After all, when it comes to matters of the heart, common sense ain't exactly top priority. Torn between two friends, his and mine, whom I'd like to see 'join forces' I've decided once and for all, it really is time to hang up my matchmaking apron. Time to step out of the affairs of others and tend to my own biscuits humming in the oven. The cupcakes I attempted to bake are tart to say the least. The bitterness is a reminder to not go trying to alter that which I cannot control. So with that said... I resign!

BEAT'CHA TO THE PUNCH BOWL

Herman's in law, a.k.a the eldest of my baby brothers, is getting married next spring. So are we, ooops didn't mean to breathe that! His date is scheduled for mid-March... darn overachiever. Just had to go and beat me to the punch. It's okay though. With all this mess and confusion of divorce, I'm in no hurry to get to the alter, I will hear those wedding bells when the time is right. But for now, pre wedded bliss it is. I still can't believe it though. Who gave my *baby* brother permission to do that? I suppose I'll let it go this time...........

ON ANOTHER NOTE: IMAGINE HIS SURPRISE

A complete and total stranger just inquired of the happily pre wedded couple, "Are you two brother and sister?" I only smiled and flashed her the 'bling, bling, bling'. Herman literally choked out a "No!" (by the way, he's always doing that... choking and carrying on, geesh, so dramatic). The question has taken him by surprise, but not me. This likeness has been brought to my attention before by friends, family members, and the occasional stranger. "Wow! You two look alike." they all claim. So I'm not surprised. Just riddled with laughter at his response

SLEEP NEVER COMES GENTLY

I have what you would call a classic case of insomnia. Self-diagnosed of course. I don't exactly need a doctor telling me what I already know... I, can't sleep! I don't believe it's anything medical. I'm quite certain that the issue is mental. My mind wired, kicks into overdrive at the strike of 12 each night. I'm writing, reading, typing, surfing the internet and everything aside from sleeping. Call it strange but I concentrate best when my family is resting. Uninterrupted minutes turn into hours. It always feels great to get so much done, except that it feels so bad knowing that by the time I lay my head down, the sun is coming up and the birds are chirping and with that the dawn of a new day and the onset of my insomniac ways begin again.

<u>MY PHOBIA</u>

It's not that dreaded insomnia, nightmares that reoccur, or babbling incoherently in my sleep (most of my fears revolve around slumber). No it's none of these things. The fear that ridicules me daily is the fear of losing my engagement ring, or um uh, my bling! The beautifully crafted, white gold, diamond embezzled bling, bling, bling. The thought has occurred to take it off before rest and place it back upon my finger with the dawn of a new day. But even that terrifies me! What if I forget where I put it, or what if one of the kiddos should come across it in passing and decide to try it on, over the sink, and it falls down down down the drain. The fear of losing my ring is worse than any nightmare. Not that I'm so attached and materialistic in any way, but I guess it's embedded somewhere in my subconscious that its existence is the most visible evidence of his love for me...

OH WHAT A TWIST

This is not the story of a good girl gone rogue for a bad boy. Instead, I can only hope my dark ways and bad influence is not contagious. Herman is beyond intrigued at my tattooed skin, my carefree whims, my ever changing long hair-short hair phases, my brash honesty, my uniqueness! I've asked just for pure curiosity, what is the thing he loves best about me; his response, "Your spontaneity." I'm certain this peppered with a good boy gone rogue for a bad girl are both to blame for the look of love in his eyes!

IF IT PLEASES THE COUNCIL

All of the 'i's have been dotted and every 't' has been crossed, and no stone has been left unturned. Yes. I came prepared! Nervous, anxious, and prepared. My sister in law to be accompanied me on this journey to freedom, imagine the irony. The trip was quick. We found parking alright. But that walk from Jade to the courtroom was agonizing. I didn't know what to expect! A courtroom full of criminals, crooks, and convicts, a jury ready to deliberate "guilty", a packing heat policeman, and a judge prepared to hurdle 'the book' at me? Instead I was met by a bailiff and a very empty courtroom. Insert anxious tension here. Then to add drama to the horror score already in progress, the bailiff walks out of the courtroom and calls down the too wide halls, for my estranged husband! I exhaled when she returned unaccompanied. She motioned for me to follow her to the judge's chambers. There I was greeted by a lady judge who seemed to understand my condition of being legally unable to move on. But even this unspoken sympathy did not save me from the law, yet again. She scheduled a 2nd hearing because my ex was a no-show, but still was due a mandated grace, during which time he could appeal! Another agonizing wait. The good news? The Judge has noted, divorce and full custody per my request the next time she and I met. I can't wait!

BAH HUMBUG

I really do hate to be a Scrooge but I loathe this time of the year. That weird climatic transition between seasons. Autumn selling tricks of optical illusions. All the gem colored leaves, everything so brisk and full of life. What a sham. So much beauty on the verge of death. All that changing in the outside world. It's no wonder all these transformations have begun to manifest themselves in the life of a bride to be. Let's see, where to start? With the self-removal of one bridesmaid, the upset of another, the noticeable distance of another? The loss of a close bond? The cancelation of tuxedos, AGAIN.!? The dress awaiting its ever impatient mistress? The never ending holidays? Jade problems? Perhaps I should start with the bills of a real Atlanta housewife... With Thanksgiving and Christmas on the heel of one another, it's no wonder I've turned into Ebenezer. I imagine I'm not the only one not much in a cheerful holiday mood. I just hope that once these festivities have come to a halt, that I'm in the marrying mood; but for now Bah Humbug.

Winter

MORE THAN THE LEAVES ARE FALLING

Autumn has come to an end and I'm still attached to the other guy. That's horrible news. The good news is that the judge didn't bother checking all the red tape. She saw a sad woman ready to move on, a guy whose life still needed a little tweaking and the paperwork stating that he had been served. But even this ain't gonna speed up the process, forced to spend another holiday legally bound to another. This is really beginning to drag. I'm feeling like next year can't get here fast enough...

WOW

I suppose I hadn't given it much thought before but Herman is such a great father figure. Scratch that... He is a wonderful father. I have sat in on a few classes in an attempt to better understand my middle child's struggles in 5th grade math. But it's no secret the stuff remains a foreign language to me. Turning fractions into decimals, multiplying percentages, PORTUGESE. Seeing my frustration, the Honey has come to my rescue. Now it is he that sits beside my middle child in class and watches to get a feel for the teaching method being used so that he can understand what our daughter is missing and why, so that we can better assist her at home; all of this done when he could be snoozing. Up in the a.m., to class with her, then to work. WOW! He may not be their biological father but he's shaping up to be one hellova dad!

FRIENDSHIP IS KEY

I believe with every endeavor nothing is new, only recycled, rejuvenated, and reused. This marriage thing has been around for a loooooong time. Designed 'til death do us part!!' Well you know how I feel about that. The last marriage certainly received the death penalty. Even with all of this mess in front of me, I still honor the idea. So I've looked at those around me and have decided that what I want with him is the essence of what the older married couples have, a friendship that cannot be broken. Marriages breakdown irretrievably every day, but a best friend never leaves your side. I'm convinced this ultimately is the secret. Aside from commonality and submission, friendship is key to a long-lasting, happy marriage. I just know it.

SIMPLE ELEGANCE

With each new date we set, an alternate is marked on the calendar. Needless to say, this can be rather discouraging. My dreams are becoming more and more concrete. Who needs a dj or a band when we're the only ones that'll remember 10 years from now 'our special song'? Sometimes too much can be just that... a bit much. It's time dreams become reality. After this burden releases me I'm throwing caution to the wind once more. But this time it's for keeps. I'm thinking me, him, my parents, his sister and her family, the preacher and the Powers that Be. Oh and maybe his cousin and my bestie. Did I mention how ready I am to be finally be his wife?

THE NEVERENDING STORY

I guess I'm a little heartbroken today. It seems to me that something is forever coming up. With each new date we set, another obstacle springs forth. Needless to say, I'm over anxious about this new one! Dare I breathe it? Another delay...

SEPARATION BLUES

Lying in bed

Enjoying his presence

My nose to his face

Titillating

Intoxicating

Scent and memory combine

Mind's eye etches a

Picture that can't be

Erased

And every time he's away

I miss him

THE TASTE IS FADING

Before the ink has dried, 2 weeks before the paperwork has been signed, an ongoing chapter has been closed. I wasn't certain how soon paths of my soon to be ex-husband and myself would cross. And just as the thought occurred, I was brought face to face with my past. The sight of him has been reciprocated in a good way. No old feelings remain, anger has been replaced with forgiveness, and I'm enjoying the moment! So this is what it feels like to move on? I walked away 4 years ago, I closed the chapter today. Despite what I thought I'd feel, I'm glad! I wish him happiness as I continue my life without him. The bad taste is slowly fading! Letting go is SWEET!

ROME

Remnants of those old buildings have finally fallen. The dust has settled and what lay in its wake is something entirely new. A different bond seems to be surfacing. Out of all that heartache, pain, and misunderstanding that comes with the territory of a young 'love', an ousted fire has sparked an ember of something strange. What a nice surprise. Here I was thinking okay, I'm supposed to buy into the whole exes at each other's throat stereotype and along came a friend.

GETTING READY

Ratty Bathrobe, Jumbo Rollers, and been to hell and back' Fuzzy Slippers. Preparing for my role as WIFE.

FYI

Okay, here we go! For your information, kisses don't shut me up! They only pacify the debate for a moment. But be warned! However brief the moment, it's still just that! Arms crossed because I'm not ready to NOT be upset.

I DECLARE WAR

Informal. Formal. Quaint. Grande. Intimate. His vision... A war of the hearts has been brewing for quite some time now. Like a dormant beast, snoring gently... Sleeping heavily... Herman and I have tip toed gingerly around the slumbering beast. But it has been awakened. Three little words, "Not good enough," and World War III has commenced! A year after the initial plans were made, Herman decides the church isn't good enough! He wants big..... Bigger......Bigger-est! His sister has been enlisted to 'search' with him. With only a few short weeks to go, my fingers were secretly crossed; hoping, wishing that they wouldn't find anything! But if I don't know anything else, I know he will find a way! So we've gone from a sweet church in the heart of a charming park, to cathedral in the heart of the city! Buckhead, where else? With a change in location, a change in attire is required, a change in menu is inescapable and a change in psyche is inevitable. I'm having a hard time with all of it. He says I deserve it, that and so much more. All I'm hearing is our intimate wedding fade away......

NOT GOOD ENOUGH

Why is it my minimalist ways are seen as frugal? Why is frugal synonymous with cheap? And why is the church that we finally decided upon, all of a sudden, not good enough? I'm lost, hurt, confused. This whole scene has unfolded in a very bad way! Now I'm pondering if it's me that's not good enough. I feel this awful turmoil boiling, working its way to the surface and I just know it's a matter of time before it all spills over!

BELLS AND WHISTLES

Every bell and whistle has been employed. Okay. Just when did Herman and Plan A take effect? Every frivolous fancy you can think of is being incorporated. A cathedral with 50 foot ceilings and organ pipes embedded in the walls. A place of worship that has done away with pews and instead the main décor is stadium seating. I may be exaggerating slightly, but certainly not by much.

LETTING GO & LETTING A GOOD MAN

I'm learning that there is a time and a place for everything. And one place that is not exactly appropriate for creative control is in a relationship. I never want to come across as sneaky, conniving or manipulative when it comes to matters of the heart. I've gotta learn in lei of this, to allow his talents to show through too. Take for instance his uncanny ability for turning a ride on the town into a date. Sightseeing, dessert at a local coffee shop, checking out the newest titles on the shelves of a book store and my all-time favorite past time, perusing old things; antique and vintage things. And he knows this. So instead of being an atypical woman, I am learning to relinquish all of that creative control I've come to rather cherish, and allow him his dues in this sometimes 50/50 partnership. It's a beautiful thing when this ingenuity is shared. I suppose you can say I'm learning to submit via compromise.

HE LEADS. SHE FOLLOWS

Imagine the dynamics, it makes for a great, no, amazing 1st dance; one that is eternal. A tango of hearts! A foxtrot of souls! A salsa of two lives! I pray this dance lasts a lifetime!

GRIN & BEAR IT

Fake, phony, false. Where is it written that the pretension of all married' couples is 'To be in love is to be happy'? I vote that when all is not sunshine and rainbows on the relationship front that it is a mandatory requirement to let those not so giddy emotions show just as visibly as the elated in love so I must be happy ones. Not every day is uphill.

What fun would an all uphill roller coaster be?

So instead of putting on the mask and carrying on with the 'Grin & Bear It' charade, let the rawness of the relationship show. Love is not a facade, and those in its throes should not be afraid to show the downs of it.

MASON JAR

Wrapping a pretty ribbon around a stout mason jar. A gift from Herman and I, to a dear friend. The gift will be presented to her and her husband in celebration of their 12 year anniversary! The attached letter reads something like this:

Marriage is more than an institution. It's a mason jar. Full of all the happiness the hopefully, blissful married couple, together, puts inside! The clear outer walls of the glass mason jar is the perfect window to the outside world and all of its temptations! The same temptations that are eagerly awaiting a chance to ruin your union. But instead of a window, treat the outer glass as a shield! Protecting what's inside and keeping anything detrimental, out! Just as easily as good can be put in, it can seep out. The key is to maintain upkeep on the mason jar.

PANGS RESURFACE

There's that old headache I have come to know and loathe. Not as familiar as it once had been, his tone of voice was odd. Every statement seemed as if I were being prepared for the kill. And just as niceties were wrapping up... he pounced. He who? My ex-husband that's who.... Whoa... my EX! That feels good. Anywho, my EX-HUSBAND decides to ask if the children can spend the weekend with him, 4 ½ hours away, in the middle of the school year. There are no holidays or breaks coming up, so being the voice of reason, I declined! My assumption that he would be irate over my rank was dead on! The tone of the call changed as did the atmosphere. Then the full on inquisition and the portrayed hurt feelings. But I'm used to being the heavy. "No" is an adamant part of my vocabulary. It has to be or I'd always be pleasing others & not myself. Well this is a new day. Those pains that have threatened to resurface have little, no correct that.... They have no control. A stressed bride does not make a happy wife. Relocating my place of Zen!

DIFFERENT CREATURE

Cold feet a few hours before the wedding? That seems normal enough. But cold feet a few months before the wedding? That seems like somebody is having second thoughts. You would think that with all the dress changes, bridesmaids coming and going, and numerous dates set, that he and I would be totally cool and in control. So why then just the opposite? I'm beginning to pick up on a few subtle hints that Mr. Taylor's feet aren't just cold, they're freezing. Then again, maybe that's just my imagination. Our impending union is transforming us into very different creatures. I just hope that it's for better and not worst!

EMOTIONAL BRIDE

What happened to the tough chic with the bad ass tattoos and attitude to match? I'll tell you what happened to her..... She began the journey of a bride to be. The closer we get to that elusive date, the louder violins play. I'm half expecting to turn the corner one day and literally run into the Philharmonic Orchestra. But instead of that ol' faithful, tough as nails exterior, I'm a sniveling pre-wedding mass. Can we say, "Not cool... Not cool at all!"

REASON STEPPED IN...

and the Joneses stepped out! Or so I thought. It seems that minor details that have been altered, such as the wedding location itself, has the power to wreak havoc on the whole scene!! Not just figuratively speaking. With a larger church, the guest list has doubled in size and the reception style just went from quaint and festive to formal and stuffy. The menu needs tweaking. But this is the least of my concern. I refuse to wear some heavily beaded, cathedral type get up with all that hot, itchy under stuff and shoulder length gloves. I mean really! Who's getting married here, me or the Princess of Wales? Now I'm a nervous wreck and it's all because of him! Yes, I know he wants the best for me. Top notch. Caviar, filet mignon and all that jazz. But there's this nagging feeling in the pit of my stomach that says he is trying to impress someone! Who? Certainly not me! Perhaps the overcompensation is an effort to 'WOW'... himself! I just don't get it. These plans don't feel right. They don't seem like us. They are the furthest thing from my own personality. Put simply, I'm anything but interested in keeping pace with the Joneses. I'd much rather keep tempo with the click of my own hot pink wedding stilettos!

THE LAND OF MILK AND HONEY

Where are the magical, 'I'll take care of everything, your wedding is my command!' fairies? I assume they live in a land of milk and Honey. What do these fairies do for fun? Plant coin seeds and shake money trees, of course. What is supposed to be a well thought out festivity is turning into a self-planned fiasco.

CURTAIN CALL

The very last thing I remember is a phone call, him speaking into the receiver, "Hello. Hello. Hello?" and then he walks off. When he returns, he drops the 'O' bomb. At first I was naïve as to what was happening and the magnitude of a seemingly harmless speech. His voice wavered as he broke the bad news. "I don't think we should get married." Um, okay. I can deal with that. You want to set a new date. Too fast too soon too overwhelmed. I don't mind letting everyone know that we will be tying the knot at a later time. That's when it hit me. The thing that has changed the way I look at him. "I don't think we should get married, at all." Whoa. Talk about a curtain call.

SURREAL

Out of nowhere, this slap in the face has shocked and surprised me. This moment seems surreal. He's standing in front of me saying something, but I can't comprehend the words. I can only see his lips moving. My entire world has screeched to a halt but the floor beneath me is spinning. This can't be real. What do you mean 'over'? Why all of a sudden the change in heart and mind? Lost and confused, I can feel the breaths grow short beneath my heaving chest… And I struggle to wake from this bad dream!

LOOKING BACK

No warning signs. No sirens or alarms. No hints or clues. Sure we argue on occasion. Nothing detrimental comes of it though. No broken dishes or bruised bodies. Oh no, nothing like that. Semi loud disagreements can be heard emitting from the walls of our bedroom on occasion. But what relationship is defunct of individual personalities that at times crash into one another? Still, was that reason enough to walk away. To let the World devour, which was once in my mind, cozy and complete. Looking back, I just don't get it.

WAITING

No call. No text. No knock. No key turning in the lock. No, "Yes, I still love you!" I guess it really is over.

BREADCRUMBS

How bitter this moment. How befitting to my current mood. Not much for nourishment but knowing that I need to eat something, anything, I've walked through the grocer's aisle in a zombie like state. A hand I barely recognize, with bling still intact, reaches for a jar of cheap caviar. It is shelved between canned crab meat and Vienna sausages. Two more items round off this trip. Back home, I drank Chardonnay out of the bottle as I devoured the caviar and crackers in a trance. Absentminded, going through the motions. My heart is very much the same as the remnants of crackers which lay in my lap. Breadcrumbs. Broken. Unwhole.

GLORY BE

Could it be? My mother's words coming back to haunt me. Did I magnify the wrong name? Men always disappoint.

BRIDES AND BARS

What do they have in common? Absolutely nothing, but I'm contemplating taking the dress out, dolling my hair up, putting on those hot pink stilettos and stepping out. Destination? The nearest bar. I could care less about outlandish looks. I just want a nice, cold, tall, strongly mixed, dangerously intoxicating Amaretto Sour, or Long Island Iced Tea, or whatever the stranger next to me is having.

THE MOURNING AFTER

The trigger that sent me into mourning, my wedding dress. Stood up. Abandoned. Left. Just like me. I'm moving through the phases at neck breaking, record speed. The sad thing is, each emotion is on constant repeat. My emotions were severed and my feelings have been amputated from my body. Numbness is setting in. It feels like I lost my bestfriend. There is an empty throbbing where I'm certain he ripped my heart from beneath my breast. These feelings, thoughts, emotions and so many more, weigh heavy on my soul. But the one sensation that overshadows them all... Anger. I'm mad as hell! I woke up feeling tired. Tired of waiting. Tired of fighting. Tired of trying to figure out what went wrong. Tired of wondering when will anyone stand and go to war for my love. My guess is, never. The clouds of self-doubt are nearing. I feel like my life has been altered indefinitely. The fairytale has been erased. My spirit weak, struggling to hold on. The only thing my feet know to do is stay. One thing I'm not by far is a coward. I have in me a strength to survive all things. But this pain is unreal and unbearable. It can't belong to me. But the tears on my pillow say otherwise. He claims promises made will be kept. Today I'm still not sure. Will there be a new diary? Well, I guess that too shall be seen. But for now, this is The End.

THE DIARY OF A BRIDE TO BE

BOOK 3

H.E.A

Happily Ever After

KATANDRA SHANEL JACKSON

H.E.A

You ever look up a word seeking clarification, only to be bombarded by a zillion definitions? Happily ever after! Perhaps 'Happily ever after...' is lush green grass, wrap around porches, the smell of freshly baked cookies and white picket fences. Perhaps 'Happily ever after...' is finally putting on that white dress, walking down the aisle and making a forever commitment to the love of your life. Then again, who's to say 'Happily ever after...' isn't freedom? Unadulterated, happy-go-lucky, blissful, without a care in the word, freedom? As I open the pages of a new diary, I can honestly say, I don't know what's in store for me, and although I have high expectations, my umbrella is near and I'm always prepared. Come whatever bight skies or storms that may, The Diary of A Bride To Book 3 begins, H.E.A.

AUTHOR BIO

Katandra Shanel Jackson is the proud Chief Everything Officer at FreedomInk Publishing! Throughout her day, she dons many hats, steps into many roles, and oversees the production of a plethora of simultaneous projects. By the end of summer 2012, FreedomInk will have published 8 books, The Diary of A Bride To Be Books 1 & 2, are amongst those titles.

In addition to FreedomInk, Katandra is the Founder of The Angel Eyes Foundation. The purpose in this social advocacy platform is to raise and promote awareness on the dangers of child sexual abuse, online and in the community. The Author/Publisher resides in Atlanta Georgia with her three children.

www.ingramcontent.com/pod-product-compliance
Lightning Source LLC
LaVergne TN
LVHW011913080426
835508LV00007BA/507